FEB   2003

Robert Jarvik and the First Artificial Heart

John Bankston

Mitchell Lane
PUBLISHERS

PO Box 619
Bear, Delaware 19701

Unlocking the Secrets of Science

Profiling 20th Century Achievers in Science, Medicine, and Technology

Robert Jarvik and the First Artificial Heart

· ·

Copyright © 2003 by Mitchell Lane Publishers, Inc. All rights reserved. No part of this book may be reproduced without written permission from the publisher. Printed and bound in the United States of America.

First Printing

Library of Congress Cataloging-in-Publication Data

Bankston, John, 1974-
    Robert Jarvik and the first artificial heart/John Bankston.
        p. cm.-- (Unlocking the secrets of science)
    Includes bibliographical references and index.
    ISBN 1-58415-116-1
    1. Jarvik, Robert, 1946- 2. Heart, Artificial. 3. Heart, Mechanical. 4. Surgeons--Biography. 5. Heart--Surgery--History. I. Title. II. Series.
RD598.35.A78 B363 2001
617.4'120592—dc21
    [B]
                                            2001050448

ABOUT THE AUTHOR: Born in Boston, Massachusetts, John Bankston began publishing articles in newspapers and magazines while still a teenager. Since then, he has written over two hundred articles, and contributed chapters to books such as *Crimes of Passion* and *Death Row 2000*, which have been sold in bookstores around the world. He has recently written a number of biographies for Mitchell Lane including books on Mandy Moore, Jessica Simpson and Jonas Salk. He currently lives in Los Angeles, California, pursuing a career in the entertainment industry. He has worked as a writer for the movies Dot-Com and the upcoming *Planetary Suicide*, which begins filming in 2002. As an actor John has appeared in episodes of *Sabrina the Teenage Witch*, *Charmed* and *Get Real* along with appearances in the films *Boys and Girls*, and *America So Beautiful*. He has a supporting part in *Planetary Suicide* and has recently completed his first young adult novel, *18 To Look Younger*.

PHOTO CREDITS: cover: Scott Rathburn; p. 6 Scott Rathburn; p. 12 Hank Morgan/ Photo Researchers; p. 18 Bettmann/Corbis; p. 24 Bettmann/Corbis; p. 31 Bettmann/ Corbis; p. 32 Bettmann/Corbis; p. 36 Hank Morgan/Photo Researchers; p. 42 Scott Rathburn; p. 44 Scott Rathburn.

PUBLISHER'S NOTE: In selecting those persons to be profiled in this series, we first attempted to identify the most notable accomplishments of the 20th century in science, medicine, and technology. When we were done, we noted a serious deficiency in the inclusion of women. For the greater part of the 20th century science, medicine, and technology were male-dominated fields. In many cases, the contributions of women went unrecognized. Women have tried for years to be included in these areas, and in many cases, women worked side by side with men who took credit for their ideas and discoveries. Even as we move forward into the 21st century, we find women still sadly underrepresented. It is not an oversight, therefore, that we profiled mostly male achievers. Information simply does not exist to include a fair selection of women.

Contents

In his quest to make an artificial heart, Dr. Robert Jarvik has developed the Jarvik 2000, a heart he believes is truly "forgettable."

Chapter 1

Straight to the Heart

• •

You put your hand over it whenever you pledge allegiance to the flag of the United States of America. You cross it when you make a promise. It aches when you're sad, breaks when things are really bad, but overflows when you're especially glad.

It's your heart, and although it's an organ that is just about the size of your fist and weighs only about ten ounces, it does an enormous amount of work. Every minute, it pumps an average of sixty to one hundred times per minute, sending blood which contains life-giving oxygen through the literally thousands of miles of blood vessels that reach every nook and cranny in your body. In one year the human heart can beat over thirty million times, or 2,000,000,000 (that's two BILLION) times in an average life span.

The heart lies close to the center of the chest, located just between the lungs. Most people think they are placing their hand over it when their finger tips are just above the lower left portion. This is the section of the heart you can feel beating.

Your heart is enclosed inside a thin layer of tissue called the pericardium. The pericardium is tough on the outside to protect the heart from damaging itself by rubbing against your lungs and chest wall. Yet the inside has a smooth lining that secretes a slippery liquid film so that when the heart beats it doesn't cause any friction, which might cause it to wear out prematurely.

It's divided into two chambers, which are separated vertically by a layer of muscle called the septum. The chambers in turn are divided into an upper and a lower section. Each upper section is called an atrium, while the lower sections are known as ventricles.

The atria (plural of atrium) collect blood as it returns from its journey through your body. The heartbeat cycle begins when the atria walls contract, which forces blood into the ventricles. Then the ventricles contract, which forces blood out into your body. Then the heart relaxes, which allows blood to flow into the atria and the process starts all over again.

The atria walls are relatively thin. The ventricles, on the other hand, have thick muscular walls because they have to pump blood throughout your body. The right ventricle supplies blood to the nearby lungs, while the left ventricle pumps blood throughout the rest of your body. Because that blood has so much further to travel, the walls of the left ventricle are three times thicker than the ones on the right ventricle.

The basic system is very simple. Blood first is pumped to the lungs, where it picks up oxygen that you inhale with every breath and at the same time gets rid of carbon dioxide. Then it returns to the heart, where it's pumped out again to carry that vital oxygen so that all the trillions of cells in your body can share in its vitality.

If you're doing something calm, such as sleeping or sitting at a desk and reading, your heart beats normally at about sixty to eighty times a minute. But if you're doing something active like running fast, then your body needs much more oxygen. You start to breathe a lot more heavily and your heart beats much more rapidly, sometimes as often as 200 times a minute or even more.

This action drives blood through the blood vessels, from the thick arteries (which carry oxygen-rich blood) to the smaller veins (which bring blood back to the heart) and tiny capillaries (which reach all the cells in your body). These blood vessels are like the body's highway system, the blood cells like delivery trucks transporting oxygen from the lungs and returning with waste: carbon dioxide which is exhaled, or breathed out, from the lungs.

As you can see, the heart is an amazing organ, far more efficient than any machine that human beings have ever created. Most of us take our heart for granted, hardly ever giving it a second thought. It works quietly and dependably.

But if something happens to your heart, the entire body suffers very quickly. A person is usually declared brain-dead if his heart stops beating for just five minutes. Every year nearly one million people in the United States die from heart disease, making it the nation's leading killer.

So it's not surprising that for over one hundred years, people have tried to construct replacement hearts so that even a person with a diseased heart can have a better chance of living.

Henry Martin crafted a blood pumping machine in 1880. Forty-eight years later, E.H.J. Schuster and H.H. Dale built their own pump to move blood through an animal without its own heart. Even the famous transatlantic pilot Charles Lindbergh, in collaboration with the famous surgeon and Nobel Prize winner Alexis Carrel, built a heart machine called the Lindbergh Pump in the 1930s after his sister-in-law developed a serious heart condition.

But despite some progress, none of these pioneers was able to successfully replace the human heart.

By the 1960s, there was also progress in the field of heart transplants, the process of replacing a diseased or damaged organ with a healthy one. Although heart transplants are now being done on a fairly regular basis, patients whose hearts are no longer functioning often must wait a long time for transplants. This wait is life-threatening. Providing a man-made organ during this time period could save lives.

Human beings have imagined building or transplanting organs for thousands of years. Four thousand years ago, Egyptian warriors grafted healthy skin onto their injured faces. In 1812, Julian Jean C'sar La Gallois proposed constant blood injections for victims of heart failure.

Six years later, English author Mary Shelley's novel *Frankenstein* imagined a man-like creature created by spare parts. In the novel's conclusion, his death occurred in a dramatic fashion. In the real world, the first patients to receive transplanted and artificial organs also died, often after long periods of suffering. Despite these setbacks, the promise of saving a patient's life from an implanted organ was compelling enough to drive doctors and scientists to pursue transplants and artificial organs throughout the twentieth century.

Eventually a number of medical pioneers succeeded in transplanting organs, including the heart. Man-made hearts have been less successful.

This is the story of one man who tried to overcome those odds. He was the son of a prominent surgeon and only became interested in medicine when heart disease nearly killed his father. Rejected by over a dozen medical schools, he left the United States to study in Italy and worked in a New York medical supply house. His opportunity to be on the forefront of artificial heart development began when he was hired as a lab assistant earning just one hundred dollars a week. He dreamed of creating an artificial heart. He hoped some day a man-made heart could save the lives of people like his father.

His name is Robert Jarvik, and this is his story.

Attractive and personable, Dr. Robert Jarvik was the perfect spokesperson for the controversial artificial heart program.

Chapter 2

Facing Rejection

Modern surgery is often performed in "operating theatres," rooms with rows of seating in a balcony where operations can be observed. It's a chance for medical students to learn new skills and for even experienced doctors to see innovative techniques.

In the late 1950s and early 1960s, Dr. Eugene Jarvik often performed surgery in front of an audience. In the midst of the observing doctors and medical students, there was often a teenager, standing alone. He was a good-looking kid, slight of build with dark hair; sometimes he asked better questions than the med students.

His name was Robert Jarvik and he was the doctor's son.

Robert Koffler Jarvik was born in Midland, Michigan on May 11, 1946 to Dr. Jarvik and his wife Edythe. Shortly afterwards, Robert moved with his family to Stamford, Connecticut, a leafy upscale suburb where his father became a prominent surgeon.

Dr. Eugene Jarvik was renowned for his skills in the operating room. Young Robert inherited one of his father's talents: manual dexterity, or the ability to work well with your hands. Medical students who want to become successful surgeons often practice a variety of complicated finger exercises, from rolling a quarter from finger to finger like a magician to sewing careful stitches without looking.

As a teenager, Robert even occasionally assisted his father with operations.

Although Robert was comfortable around surgical procedures and skilled with his hands, he had little interest in medicine.What Robert Jarvik loved was building things.

In an interview with *People Weekly*, Robert Jarvik recalled that he was "a kid who was always mentally disassembling things and putting them back together."

Back when he was in elementary school, Robert was like many other boys his age. He built model ships and airplanes. However, as he grew older, Robert began to imagine creating things which would fill a need, or correct a problem. Considering solutions to existing problems is often the first step for a budding inventor.

It was during all the times that he watched his father perform surgery that Robert first considered a medical invention.During those operations that Robert observed, his father had to manually clamp and tie off blood vessels. It was a time-consuming procedure, and Robert understood that in a delicate operation the longer a patient is in surgery the more dangerous the operation becomes. So he began considering a ways in which he could help to speed up the process, getting the patient in and out of the operating room more rapidly.

"It seemed to me that there was a better way to close wounds than by sewing," he said in an interview with *Newsweek* magazine. His curiosity soon led him to an ordinary device—the stapler. He believed that just as an office stapler can connect pieces of paper, a surgical stapler could be designed to bind blood vessels to each other.

It didn't take him long to create such a device. So before Robert Jarvik had even graduated from high school, he owned the patent for an automatic surgical stapler. This means no one else could copy his idea and sell it without Robert's permission. But despite this impressive achievement, he still had no interest in pursuing a career in medicine.

In 1964, Robert entered Syracuse University in upstate New York, where he studied everything from architecture to sculpting.

"I'm not a conventional thinker," Jarvik admitted to *Fortune* magazine, "and as an undergraduate... I never really put my effort into what I was supposed to do." Because of this lack of effort, Robert Jarvik's grades were terrible. Still, Robert's father never pressured his son to pursue medicine. Indeed it was never what Dr. Eugene Jarvik *said* which influenced Robert. Instead, it was what his father *survived* which changed Robert Jarvik's career path. When Robert was still a student at Syracuse, his father developed an aortic aneurysm. That is an abnormal enlargement of the blood vessel called the aorta, the largest in the human body. It nearly killed him and meant that he had to undergo a major heart operation.

During his father's recovery from heart surgery in 1965, Robert made a life-altering choice. He switched his major to zoology, which put him on an educational track geared toward enrollment in medical school after graduation.However, that didn't mean that Robert abandoned his passion for invention.

To Robert, the disease affecting his father was more than a life-threatening ailment which killed thousands of people every year. It was also a problem to solve. He realized that solving the problem of heart disease was far more complicated than inventing a surgical stapler. In order to invent a solution, Robert Jarvik would first have to become a doctor.

In 1968, when he graduated from Syracuse University with a Bachelor of Arts degree in zoology, Robert was looking forward to beginning his training as a doctor. Unfortunately, his poor study habits interfered with his ambition. Even though he applied to over a dozen medical schools, they all rejected him.

Robert was forced to face reality. His previous choices as a young man might mean that he wouldn't be able to pursue his dreams. But instead of giving up, he chose to do what many pre-med students do after being rejected by medical schools in the United States. He left the country.

Robert Jarvik moved to Italy to study at the University of Bologna. It was a risky choice, because a number of Americans often find it difficult to find work back in this country after graduating from foreign medical schools. Still, at the time he believed it was the best decision, maybe even the only decision that was available to him.

Leaving the United States wasn't the only change in his life. On October 5, 1968 Robert married Elaine Levin, a journalist. According to her, Robert's interest in matters of the heart reached beyond just the medical. During the couple's engagement, Elaine Levin recalls how Robert drove all the way to Alaska just so he could pan for gold. Because he was so gifted with his hands, he used the gold to fashion a wedding ring.

While his personal life seemed on track, his educational life was far less promising. Although he spent two years at the University of Bologna, Robert left without graduating. Instead he and his young bride returned to New York state. But despite the time he'd spent studying in Italy, Robert was still unable to get into medical schools. So he enrolled in New York University to study occupational biomechanics. He earned a Master of Arts degree in 1971. By then he was working at Ethicon, Inc., which was a medical supply house. The company would soon offer Robert Jarvik the opportunity he needed.

Robert's boss at Ethicon had a business connection with the University of Utah's Institute for Biomedical Engineering and Division of Artificial Organs. If Robert was able to secure a job in the Institute's laboratory, Ethicon would pay his salary.

Even better than the job was the fact that the University of Utah had a fine medical school. Working at the Institute might improve Robert's hope for medical school enrollment. There was another advantage as well. Becoming a resident of the state of Utah would mean lower tuition if he was able to be admitted to medical school there. It seemed like the chance of a lifetime.

Unfortunately, getting the job wouldn't be easy. Robert lacked formal medical training. He didn't have a background in research. And he would have to be approved by Dr. Willem Kolff, the man everyone referred to as the "pioneer of spare parts medicine."

Dr. Willem Kolff (left), the pioneer of 'spare parts medicine' assembled a top-notch team for his artificial heart program, including Dr. William DeVries (right). Dr. DeVries began working on the artificial heart as a first-year medical student and went on to perform the first artificial heart operation, with Dr. Robert Jarvik as his assistant.

Chapter 3
Spare Parts Pioneer

• •

In 1957, Dr. Willem Kolff watched sadly as a dog lay dying. As a recipient of the world's first artificial heart, the unfortunate creature barely survived ninety minutes.

Still, Dr. Kolff knew the experiment wasn't a complete failure. After all, the dog had lived through the operation. Besides, years of medical research and development had taught the doctor one thing: Experiments which don't work are necessary on the road to success. To skeptical colleagues, the doctor was fond of quoting William of Orange—the King of England at the end of the seventeenth century—who said, "Even without hope you shall undertake, and even without success you shall persevere."

Like Robert Jarvik, Dr. Kolff was the son of a doctor. Born in Holland in 1911, Kolff had survived the German occupation of his country during World War II. Despite the war and its tragedies, the doctor poured his energy into a life beyond the conflict. He found a focus for his medical training early in the war on the day he watched as a 22-year-old patient slowly died from kidney failure.

From then on, Dr. Kolff devoted himself to preventing other people from suffering the same fate. In 1943, he used some cellophane tubing, a small electric motor inside an enamel drum with a rotating tank and water seals ripped from a Ford automobile to construct the world's first working artificial kidney. It was a failure at first. Dr. Kolff lost 16 patients to the contraption, though all of them were people who were terminally ill and would have died anyway. Then finally, after three years of watching kidney patients die, he used the machine to save the life of a 67-year-old woman.

Dr. Kolff had invented the world's first functioning kidney dialysis machine. It was a prototype for equipment that is still being used to save the lives of kidney patients today, nearly sixty years later.

His success with a kidney machine convinced him of the potential for other artificial organs. Immigrating to the United States in 1950, Dr. Kolff began working on a heart-lung machine at Ohio's Cleveland Clinic. Meanwhile, in Detroit, Michigan, F.D. Dodrill built an experimental mechanical heart under the supervision of General Motors Research Division. In 1952, the device kept a patient alive during the one-hour surgery on his heart. His development paved the way for the types of heart-lung machines now used during open heart surgery.

Wanting to be an innovator, not an imitator, Dr. Kolff moved from his work on a heart-lung machine to focusing on the construction of an artificial heart. He built the first version fairly quickly and in 1957 implanted it in the dog. Despite the animal's death, Dr. Kolff believed he was making progress. Yet no matter what new methods and machinery he used, every experiment had the same conclusion: the death of the patient.

Ten years later, Dr. Kolff left Cleveland for Salt Lake City, where he organized the University of Utah's Division of Artificial Organs and was named Director of the Institute for Biomedical Engineering.

During two decades of development, work on the artificial heart was exasperatingly slow. The factors which kept people from building an artificial heart were quite different from the issues faced by the pioneers of kidney research or the heart lung machine. For one thing, Dr. Kolff's initial idea was that the device would be implanted whole in a patient's chest. That meant not only did a working heart have to be constructed, but also that the new organ would also require its own source of power.

This was a challenge, because the many millions of times that the heart would beat required an enormous amount of energy. For a while, Dr. Kolff even considered powering the heart with plutonium. One of the most dangerous substances on earth, it's powerful enough to provide the fuel for a nuclear bomb. To many people, the idea of implanting such a deadly radioactive substance into a patient's heart seemed almost insane. Only when the government stepped in and threatened to withdraw the Institute's funding did Dr. Kolff abandon this scheme.

Shortly after that fiasco, Dr. Kolff realized the idea of creating a power source small enough to fit inside a patient's chest cavity was foolhardy. Instead he decided that the machine which would power an artificial heart would have to be outside the body. The device would only replace the heartbeat, substituting for the ventricles—the organ's lower pumping chambers.

According to the 1985 edition of Melvin Berger's *Current Biography Yearbook,* "In general, the successful artificial heart would need to be small in size, durable and dependable, and yet gentle in its action upon the circulatory system."

At the Institute for Biomedical Engineering, Dr. Kolff began assembling a team to achieve those goals. He hired

Dr. Clifford Kwan-Gett, who quickly became one of the Institute's top designers. In 1971, he developed a flexible rubber diaphragm—like a skin— that would force blood in and out of the artificial heart when activated by compressed air. By 1972, animals implanted with Dr. Kwan-Gett's device were surviving up to two weeks. The device itself continued to function even after the animal's demise. The problem was that clots—or clumps of blood—were forming on the membrane and eventually causing death.

Dr. Kolff began looking to new solutions to his old problem.

In this quest, Dr. Kolff didn't just hire top medical school graduates. He brought anyone with a passion for creating into the program. In 1967, he hired William DeVries, a first-year medical student who would eventually become a top surgeon with the Institute.

In 1971, Robert Jarvik arrived to interview for a job at the Institute. Jarvik had two motivations for wanting to join Dr. Kolff's program. First, he believed working on something as complex as developing a functional artificial heart would improve his chances for admission to medical school. Second, as he admitted to *People Weekly*, "I knew that my father was going to die of heart disease, and I was trying to make a heart for him."

Despite his willingness to consider unconventional candidates, Dr. Kolff barely had time for Robert Jarvik. The young man's M.A. degree in occupational biomechanics was overshadowed by his previous poor grades at Syracuse University and almost complete lack of formal training in medical research. Although a colleague of Dr. Kolff's at

Ethicon described Jarvik as "a very ingenious fellow," the Dutch doctor worried about the candidate's seeming lack of focus in his life.

And then, a little quirk bought Jarvik the job. As he recalled in a later interview with the *Wall Street Journal*, "Dr. Kolff asked what kind of car I drove. I said I had a Volvo, his car. And he changed his mind."

Robert Jarvik was hired in 1971 as a lab assistant, pretty much the lowest position available. The salary was barely one hundred dollars a week, which wasn't very much money even at that time. But despite the low wages, the job would help to change Jarvik's life forever.

This calf, named Alfred Lord Tennyson, was kept alive by Dr. Robert Jarvik's artificial heart device, the Jarvik 7, for a record 268 days.

Chapter 4

Building a Better Heart

· ·

By the early 1970s, Robert Jarvik's life began to turn around. Before that, he'd been struggling as medical school after medical school rejected him. By his account, over the years more than twenty-five stateside programs rejected his application. Finally, in 1972, he was accepted by the University of Utah's medical school.

There were still obstacles for Jarvik. The Utah program refused to honor the credits he'd earned in Italy at the University of Bologna. The two years he'd already spent studying medicine in a foreign country never existed as far as the University of Utah was concerned.

Jarvik stayed focused despite the setback. After all, he wasn't the average first-year medical student. He'd been working on developing an artificial heart for a year when he was admitted.

"It was rather interesting as a young man to be given the opportunity to design a completely new artificial heart," Jarvik told Scott Rathburn at *CNC Machining* magazine. "I was presented with a problem and given the opportunity to solve it... Within the first six to eight months, we broke the world record for survival with one of my first designs."

Although he was barely 25, the design would have his name on it. The device he built, the Jarvik 3, was never intended for use in people. Instead it was constructed for the chest cavities of the experimental lab animals, mainly calves and sheep, at the Institute for Biomedical Engineering.

Jarvik made many alterations to the initial designs of his colleague, Dr. Clifford Kwan-Gett, including adding multiple layers of a smooth polyurethane for the device's diaphragm. The change Jarvik made would help prevent clotting, the problem which had led to early deaths for a number of the lab animals. Instead of relying on rubber for the diaphragm, Jarvik used biomer—an elastic similar to Lycra, the material found today in everything from girdles to sportswear.

Jarvik's improvement meant the calves who received his device lived for up to ninety days. It was huge step.

Medical research, like many other aspects of scientific discovery, is based in part on competition among various teams of scientists devoted to a single goal. This usually leads to discoveries occurring at a faster pace. The Utah team was racing against two other prestigious medical programs: the Baylor-Rice Artificial Heart Program in Houston, Texas and the Pennsylvania State University Division of Artificial Hearts in Hershey, Pennsylvania. Already, the work at Houston had taken a giant leap forward when Dr. Denton Cooley implanted an artificial heart into a human being during a transplant operation back in 1969.

Despite the work at Baylor-Rice, Jarvik's work quickly outshone all other programs. While Dr. Cooley *had* used his heart on a human being, the device was only in operation for an hour before his patient received a transplant.

The Jarvik 3 was keeping animals alive for three months!

Reporters and other members of the media began to descend on the program in Salt Lake City, Utah. They regularly interviewed the handsome young medical student whose device bore his name and the Dutch doctor who headed the program. And then the reporters would ask Dr. Willem Kolff the same question: When would the device be ready for human beings?

And Dr. Kolff had ready the same answer: "I will be disappointed if the artificial heart is not ready in three years, and three years ago I said the same thing."

The lessons learned from the Jarvik 3 led to design changes which evolved into the Jarvik 7. Robert Jarvik and the rest of the Utah team knew *this* was the one, this was the device that would someday replace a human heart!

The Jarvik 7 consisted of dacron polyester, aluminum and plastic. It was only slighter larger than a human's fist-sized heart, and at ten ounces, weighed about the same. Like the previous models, it had two artificial ventricles, similar to the pumping chambers of the heart. The device was designed to be attached to the patient's atria, the upper chambers of the heart which receive blood from the veins. As with the other devices, it would be powered by the compressed air from an outside device connected to the patient's chest through tubes.

By the middle 1970s, Robert Jarvik's device was being tested on animals. Among them, a calf the team dubbed Alfred Lord Tennyson survived a record 268 days with the device.

It was a heady time for Robert Jarvik.

In 1976, he finally earned the M.D. degree he'd been striving towards for years. Sadly, Dr. Robert Jarvik's pleasure in his own accomplishment was short lived.

His father, Dr. Norman Eugene Jarvik finally succumbed to heart disease. "He died the year I graduated," Dr. Jarvik recalled for *CNC Machining.* "But that personal motivation was only part of the reason for working on something with a very broad need. And certainly, after he died of heart disease, I wanted the artificial heart to succeed all the more."

Progress in testing the Jarvik 7 continued, and the man who developed it saw his professional life improve as well. The former one hundred dollar a week lab assistant became a prime associate in Dr. Willem Kolff's new company, Kolff Associates, later renamed Kolff Medical, Inc.

The company's goal was to raise investor money for the private development of artificial hearts. Dr. Kolff was less interested in figuring out a way to profit from the invention than he was in insuring that the program's money wouldn't be subject to government officials changing their mind about funding. He'd already seen how a single misstep on the program's part led to the government's threatened withdrawal of financial support. Remembering what happened after he suggested plutonium power for the artificial heart, Dr. Kolff wanted to ensure the program continued to run even if the United States government someday removed its support.

Dr. Kolff didn't just hire Dr. Robert Jarvik because of his inventing skill. Dr. Jarvik would also be instrumental in attracting investors. Personable and good looking, Dr. Jarvik was more skillful at promotion than most scientists. In the

1980s, his picture would even grace advertisements for shirts; in the early days of Dr. Kolff's company, Jarvik was regularly interviewed by the press.

Still, the new company took a long time to mature. It was, as Dr. Jarvik told *Money* magazine, "a start up with a very long start up phase... very long."

In addition to his work with the new company, Dr. Jarvik began teaching at the University of Utah School of Medicine. In 1979 he was hired as a research assistant professor of surgery and bioengineering.

Meanwhile, Dr. Kolff submitted a proposal to the Food and Drug Administration, which had to approve the artificial heart before it could be implanted in human beings.

But the FDA rejected his proposal. Cardiologist Melvin Cheitlin, a member of the FDA advisory board, explained the FDA's decision by saying that the board believed artificial hearts should only be used to assist patients, not to replace their own organs entirely. As Dr. Cheitlin told *Time* Magazine, "Once you've taken someone's heart out, you've really burnt the bridge."

Dr. Kolff submitted another proposal. This time, in September 1981, the FDA approved the artificial heart for use in a human patient.

The FDA rules were very strict. The patient had to be over 18, and couldn't be eligible for a heart transplant or someone who would survive being taken off of a heart-lung machine following open heart surgery. The FDA requirements meant that the team at Utah had to seek out a so-called "Class IV" patient.

That meant that they needed to find someone who was about to die.

It took them over a year to find the right candidate. The doctors involved, including Dr. Jarvik and surgeon Dr. DeVries, used the time to carefully prepare themselves. They practiced the operation regularly, leaving nothing to chance.

So when the patient who fit the FDA's criteria appeared, the team was ready.

Dr. Barney Clark was a retired Seattle, Washington dentist who was slowly dying from cardiomyopathy, an irreversible, degenerative disease of the heart muscle. Dr. Clark's heart was growing weaker with every beat. There was no cure.

Dr. Clark traveled regularly to Utah to visit family members, and during one trip he was put in touch with the team at the Institute for Biomedical Engineering.

"He came down and looked at our animals, actually saw an operation and then went home because he wasn't bad enough," Dr. Chase Peterson, vice president for the University of Utah's health sciences told the *New York Times* soon after the operation was completed. "In the last week he's gotten severely worse, and last Saturday he called us and said, 'It's time.'"

On Monday, November 29, 1982, Dr. Barney Clark checked into the hospital at the University of Utah. He told reporters, "If I can make a contribution, my life will count for something."

As a medical professional, Dr. Clark realized his only other option was death. The Jarvik 7 was about to get its first human test.

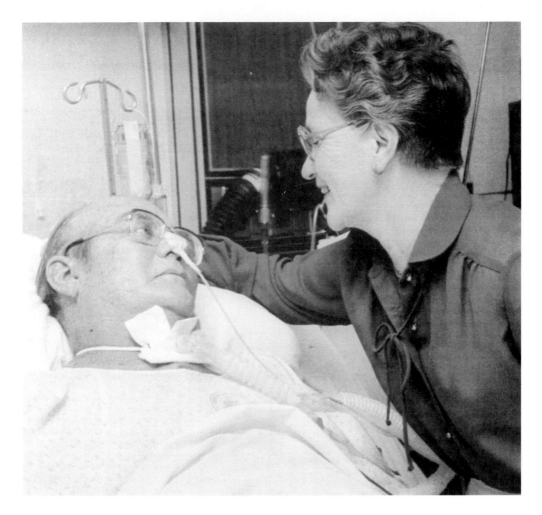

The Jarvik 7 gave terminally ill Barney Clark an extra 112 days of life, time he spent with his wife, Una Long, shown here, and his children. Though 112 days would not be considered an acceptable success rate for an artificial heart, the information and experience doctors gained from Barney Clark's operation has been used to help many other heart patients.

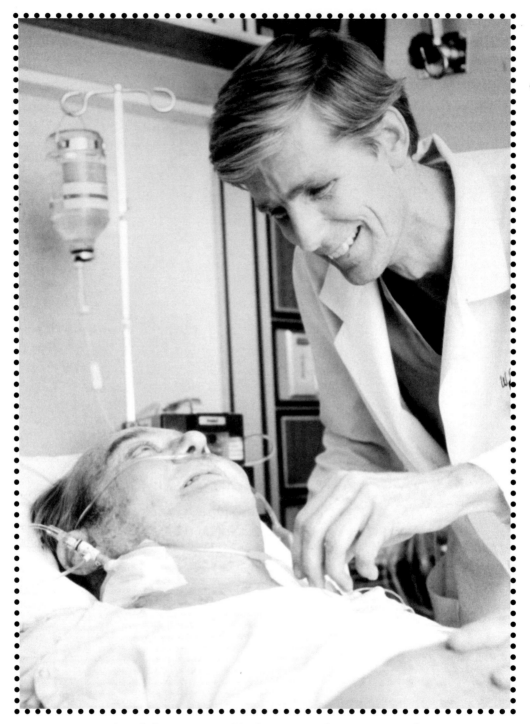

Dr. DeVries realized that Barney Clark was a "classic case in human experimentation." Despite this realization, the patient and doctor grew close during the last days of Clark's life.

Chapter 5

A Broaken Heart

●●

Just before midnight, on a snowy December morning in Salt Lake City, Utah, the pudgy former dentist was wheeled into an operating room. He was near death, his heart damaged and failing. Dr. Barney Clark was about to become a pioneer.

"This man is no different than Columbus," Dr. Peterson told the *New York Times.* "He is striking out for new territory."

During a seven and a half hour operation, 38-year-old surgeon Dr. DeVries implanted the $16,000 Jarvik 7 artificial heart into the dying man's chest. Dr. DeVries, who'd begun working with the artificial heart program when he was a first-year medical student, was assisted by Dr. Jarvik, the device's inventor.

Although Jarvik had spent his entire medical career with the program, Dr. DeVries had spent nine years at North Carolina's Duke University Medical Center because, as he admitted later to the *New York Times,* "I wanted to be with the big-time surgeons to see if I was any good."

That question was easily answered during the precedent-setting implantation. As the music of classical composer Maurice Ravel's "Bolero" pulsed from the operating room speakers, Dr. DeVries removed two thirds of Clark's damaged heart, slicing out the bottom two chambers—the left and right ventricles. The top two atria chambers of his heart were left as an anchor to which the Jarvik 7 could be attached.

Jarvik's creation was then implanted in the patient's chest. Clark, along with Dr. DeVries, Dr. Jarvik, and the artificial heart program's founder, Dr. Kolff, were described in the *New York Times* interview with Dr. Peterson as being "on the threshold of something that is as exciting and thrilling as had ever been accomplished in medicine."

"We took a patient who probably would have been dead by midnight," Dr. DeVries explained to *Newsweek*, "took him to the operating room and removed his heart. It was almost a spiritual experience for everyone in the room."

Surviving the operation was just the beginning.

As Jarvik admitted in the same *Newsweek* article, "Dr. Clark has a very difficult period ahead."

Less than two days after the operation, air bubbles caused by mild emphysema were discovered and Dr. Clark went under the surgeon's scalpel once again. It would be the first of many obstacles for the former dentist.

Twice the left ventricle had to be replaced. Dr. Clark's blood pressure plummeted several times. He would endure everything from nausea and depression to pneumonia.

Despite these burdens, there was little doubt among medical experts that without the operation Dr. Clark would not have survived the weekend. Living for him now meant being connected by six-foot tubes which exited from his chest and attached to an air compressor the doctors nicknamed "the grocery cart."

Through Clark's chest, an audible clicking sound could be heard—it was the sound of the Jarvik 7 beating, up to

120 times a minute. The clicking sound of the heart combined with the whoosh of the artificial air compressor.

It wasn't an easy existence.

But Barney Clark's decision to be a pioneer bought him time. Time with his wife, Una Long. Time with his three adult children. Dr. Clark was able to sit up in bed. He was able to speak to his wife, and hug his family. He even managed to putt around a few golf balls in his room.

Unfortunately, various complications including a bad infection in his colon and kidney failure made Dr. Clark's life after the operation very unpleasant. In *Maclean's* magazine, Dr. DeVries admitted that his patient was "a classic case in human experimentation."

For Dr. Barney Clark, there would be no recovery.

One hundred and twelve days after the operation, on March 23, 1983, Barney Clark died of multiple organ failure. His entire body shut down.

The Jarvik 7 was still beating.

Despite what many viewed as a tragic conclusion, the debut of the Jarvik 7 was positive. Prior to the operation, there were concerns about post-operative infection. This did not occur at either the site of the polyurethane heart or where the pump hoses entered Dr. Clark's chest. The pumping of the Jarvik 7 didn't damage his red blood cells. And most importantly, there were no blood clots inside the Jarvik 7. In many ways, the device had worked as well on Clark as it had on the laboratory animals.

Dr. Jarvik proudly displays the device he invented while he was still in his twenties: the Jarvik 7, a polyurethane and dacron mesh artificial heart.

Chapter 6
Fame!

∙ ∙

The life and death of Barney Clark catapulted Robert Jarvik into an elite circle of internationally known doctors and scientists. Although perhaps not quite as famous as a movie or sports star, he was still a household name. "From that moment my life changed," Jarvik later told *People Weekly*. "I was emotionally involved in the lives of the patients, and I was also traveling all over to promote the program."

The attention Jarvik received was good for his other interest: business. In 1981, Jarvik had convinced Dr. Kolff to name him president of Kolff Medical, Inc. which then became known as Symbion, Inc. Working with businessman W. Edward Massey, Dr. Jarvik began to aggressively seek funding for the venture. Following a deal with an investment firm, Jarvik restructured the company so that Dr. Kolff would no longer have managerial power. Although Dr. Kolff would still be Chairman of the Board, he'd have little actual say in the day-to-day operations of the company he'd founded.

Although they eventually reconciled, the decision would create friction between the two doctors for years. Jarvik believed he'd made the right choice, because in order for the artificial heart program to grow, it would need money. Lots of it.

"If the company were to succeed, it could not spend a lot of money playing around with a lot of impractical ideas,"

Dr. Jarvik told *Newsday*. "The company is there to succeed financially. It has to."

As to his conflict with Dr. Kolff, Dr. Jarvik went on to say, "It could be described as a father-son sort of thing, but sometimes the son revolts against the father."

For a man who'd lost his own father, the decision to basically take over Dr. Kolff's company was a difficult one.

The artificial heart program returned to the spotlight in late 1984. On November 25, William Schroeder, 52, became the second recipient of Jarvik's device. The surgery, performed once again by Dr. William DeVries, occurred this time at the Humana Hospital-Audubon in Louisville, Kentucky. Dr. DeVries had left the non-profit University of Utah for the hospital's Humana Heart Institute, which had provided some funding for Symbion. He cited the University of Utah's "red tape" as the main reason for leaving. Since Dr. DeVries was the only doctor the FDA would allow to perform the operation, when he left the artificial heart program basically left with him.

For William Schroeder, the operation was as necessary as it had been for Barney Clark. Like Clark, Schroeder was a "Class IV," a patient near death. Indeed, as a Catholic, William Schroeder was given the last rites just before being wheeled in for the nearly seven hour surgery.

But Schroeder did not die. He lived, sitting up and speaking to his wife Margaret not long after the operation. Unfortunately, his good health didn't last. Just 18 days later, William Schroeder suffered a stroke, most likely caused by a blood clot. For the man who developed a device designed to help prevent such an occurrence, Dr. Jarvik was upset, telling *People Weekly*, "When Bill had his stroke, I felt absolutely terrible."

Although Schroeder physically recovered from the episode, he would suffer several more strokes, until he was rendered completely non-communicative, living in a vegetative state. The Jarvik 7 continued to beat.

In August of 1986, William Schroeder died following a severe lung infection, and one final stroke. He had survived 620 days with the Jarvik 7 artificial heart, a record which still stands. Despite this accomplishment, Margaret Schroeder harbored mixed feelings about the implant. Writing in *People Weekly*, just a year after her husband's operation, she said, "If they tell you that you have a chance to live, you take that chance. Bill was a guy who would take a chance all his life...At first I thought the artificial heart would get Bill better... Bill's not an experiment, he's part of our family."

The reality of the artificial heart "experiment" and what it meant to the families involved stirred a continuing debate. Writing in the *American Medical News* just a few days before William Schroeder's surgery, Dr. David Olch asked, "Will the artificial heart benefit Schroeder as much as it benefits Jarvik, Humana and the surgical team?"

At the hospital in Kentucky, two more men were implanted with the Jarvik 7. Both of those men died from eventual complications similar to those which felled Clark and Schroeder.

"The Food and Drug Administration promptly shut the Jarvik-7 experiment down," wrote Steve Sternberg in the July 5, 2000 issue of *USA Today*. "*The New York Times* labeled the device the 'Dracula of Medical Technology.' The research all but vanished from view.

"But the hiatus was brief. Surgeons found a new use for the Jarvik 7, as a temporary bridge to a heart transplant, keeping some heart failure patients alive for weeks or months while they await a new heart."

While Dr. Robert Jarvik had originally conceived the device as a replacement for a damaged heart, its use as a bridge for those needing heart transplants has proven both safer and less controversial. Throughout the 1980s, 150 people in the United States utilized the artificial heart for that purpose.

Beginning in 1986, France's Dr. Christian Cabrol implanted dozens of the devices in patients, including one in a 40-year-old French woman who was able to walk around, carrying the Jarvik 7's power source in a small backpack.

During the time that Dr. Robert Jarvik's professional life gained attention, he admitted his personal life was in disarray. In 1985, he and his wife Elaine divorced. By then the couple had two young children, Tyler, then 11, and Kate, then 8. At the time of the divorce, Jarvik felt certain he'd remain unmarried, focused mainly on helping to raise his two children and drumming up support for his invention.

All of that changed when Jarvik read a magazine article two years later. The piece was a profile of Marilyn vos Savant, who according to the *Guinness Book of World Records* owned the world's highest IQ at 228. The test, which measures intelligence, earned her fame, book deals and her own column, "Ask Marilyn," in *Parade Magazine*.

It also earned her the attention of one the world's best known doctors.

Dr. Jarvik pestered friends for Marilyn's unlisted phone number. He called her, the two began dating and quickly fell in love. Marilyn vos Savant and Dr. Robert Jarvik married in the fall of 1987.

The best man was Thomas Gaidosh, who had been one of the first successful "bridge" patients. He was implanted with a Jarvik 7 for a few days before receiving a transplanted heart.

"I didn't expect to marry again," Dr. Jarvik told *People Weekly*, "because I didn't think there was anyone complete enough. But Marilyn is a person of a special intelligence and mental agility that you can't understand unless you know her well."

The same year he remarried, a New York firm purchased Symbion in a deal Dr. Jarvik opposed. The new owners fired the doctor. While he was hurt by their decision, he planned to put his energy towards developing a different device.

In 1990, the FDA, citing manufacturing deficiencies, withdrew their approval for use of the Jarvik 7 by Symbion.

A new heart for a new millenium. Dr. Jarvik holds the Jarvik 2000, an artificial heart designed to sit inside the left ventricle of a damaged heart.

Chapter 7
Jarvik 2000

• •

In the 1990s, working with the Texas Heart Institute and St. Luke's Episcopal Hospital in Houston, Texas, Dr. Robert Jarvik invented a new device for the heart. Rather than replacing a damaged heart, the invention—the Jarvik 2000—is placed inside a patient's left ventricle where its tiny propeller pumps up to 1500 gallons of blood a day. Weighing just two and half ounces, the device has none of the cumbersome qualities that were first associated with the Jarvik 7. Indeed, instead of a "grocery cart" compressor, the Jarvik 2000 is powered by an external battery pack weighing less than three pounds.

Currently the Jarvik 2000, as eventually became the case with its predecessor, has proven best as a "bridge" between transplants. So far, FDA approval is limiting the device to that function.

Not so the AbioCor Implantable Replacement Heart. Built in Danvers, Massachusetts by researchers at Abiomed, Inc., who began developing it around the time of Barney Clark's record-setting operation, the AbioCor is a plastic and titanium replacement heart the size of a softball that weighs about three pounds. Completely self-contained, it has an internal power source which allows it to function for up to thirty minutes on its own; the main power source comes from batteries attached to a belt. The device takes advantage of a variety of breakthroughs that have occurred in the twenty years since Barney Clark's operation.

"Comparing the Jarvik to the Abiomed heart is like comparing a fixed-wing 1920s plane to a Boeing 727, in terms of technological leaps," Dr. O.H. Frazier explained to the *Boston Globe*. The device was approved in February, 2001 by the FDA for five experimental implants. The first implant, which took place in a man in his 50s in Louisville, Kentucky on July 2, 2001 was considered to be a success by those involved.

Dr. Robert Jarvik is skeptical. His problem with the device is that it will only fit in patients over 200 pounds, eliminating many men and most women. Still, in some respects, the device is an attempt to achieve one of Dr. Jarvik's main goals.

"If the artificial heart is ever to achieve its objective," the doctor told *Scientific American* in 1981, "It must be more than a pump. It must also be functional, reliable and dependable. It must be forgettable. It has to be so good that the patient goes about their daily life and, most of the time, doesn't think about the fact that they have an artificial heart."

The work, begun by Dr. Willem Kolff nearly half a century ago and continued by Dr. Robert Jarvik, has led to a world where the dreams of a "forgettable" artificial heart are closer than ever .

Manufacturing the Jarvik 2000 at CNC Machining may some day be as common as producing any other medical device.

Robert Jarvik Chronology

1946, born May 11 in Midland, Michigan to Norman and Edythe Jarvik

1963, receives patent for automatic stapler

1964, enters Syracuse University, majoring in architecture and mechanical drawing

1965, changes major after father suffers near-fatal aortic aneurysm

1968, graduates from Syracuse University with a B.A. in zoology

1968, marries Elaine Levin, a journalist

1968, rejected by over a dozen medical schools, applies to the University of Bologna but leaves after two years without medical degree

1970, moves back to New York, begins working at medical supply house Ethicon, Inc.

1971, receives M.A. in occupational biomechanics from New York University

1971, accepts position as lab assistant at University of Utah's Division of Artificial Organs and the Institute for Biomedical Engineering.

1972, enters University of Utah's college of medicine

1972, designs his first artificial heart, the Jarvik 3

1976, receives his M.D. Degree from University of Utah's college of medicine, begins working full time at the Institute.

1976, becomes prime associate in artificial organs research firm, Kolff Associates, begun by Willem Kolff

1979, becomes research assistant professor of surgery and bioengineering at University of Utah's college of medicine.

1981, becomes President of Kolff Associates, now named Symbion, Inc.

1982, assists with artificial heart operation, as surgeon Dr. William DeVries implants heart into Barney Clark

1985, divorces wife Elaine

1987, marries Marilyn vos Savant

1987, fired from Symbion Corporation

1990s, develops the Jarvik 2000

Artificial Heart Timeline

1812, Julian Jean Cesar La Gallois suggests that a continuing injection of blood could keep someone whose heart has failed alive

1880, Henry Martin builds a "heart lung preparation," a machine designed to pump blood through the organs

1928, E.H.J. Schuster and H.H. Dale announce the construction of a pump to circulate blood through an animal without its own heart

1930s, Transatlantic pilot Charles Lindbergh and Dr. Alexis Carrel market their "Lindbergh" pump

1952, General Motors' researcher F.D. Dodrill uses a mechanical heart to keep a patient alive for nearly an hour during surgery

1952, Dr. Charles Hufnagel develops a plastic aortic valve

1957, Dr. Willem Kolff builds the world's first artificial heart and uses it to keep a dog alive for 90 minutes

1969, Dr. Denton Cooley implants an artificial heart developed by the team at the Baylor-Rice Artificial Heart Program. The heart is used temporarily while the patient waits for a transplant

1971, Clifford Kwan-Gett develops an artificial heart at the University of Utah, which eventually keeps animals alive for up to two weeks

1972, Robert Jarvik develops the Jarvik 3; animals implanted with the device live up to four months

1976, the Jarvik 7, an improvement on the Jarvik 3, keeps a calf alive for a record 268 days

1981, Jarvik 7 is approved for human implantation

1982, Jarvik 7 is implanted into Barney Clark, and he survives for several months

1984, Jarvik 7 is implanted into William Schroeder, who lives for nearly two years

1990, FDA removes approval of Jarvik 7 for human implantation

1990s, Robert Jarvik begins developing the Jarvik 2000, a "heart assist" device

2001, a new type of artificial heart, which doesn't require a bulky power source, is implanted in a man in Louisville, Kentucky

For Further Reading

Books:

Berger, Melvin. *The Artificial Heart.* New York: Franklin Watts, 1987.

Chung, Edward K. *One Heart, One Life.* Englewood Cliffs, NJ: Prentice Hall, 1982.

Comroe, Julius H. *Exploring the Heart.* New York: Norton, 1983.

DeBakey, Michael E. and Antonio Gotto. *The Living Heart.* New York: McCay, 1977.

Fox, Renee and Judith Swazey. *Spare Parts: Organ Replacement in American Society.* New York: Oxford University Press, 1992.

Shaw, Margery W. ed. *After Barney Clark.* Austin, TX: University of Texas Press, 1984

On the Web:

http://health.excite.com

www.tmc.edu

www.msnbc.compar RJARVIK@JARVIKHEART.COM

Glossary

aorta - The body's main artery, it carries blood from the heart's left ventricle to the entire body, except the lungs

artery - thick blood vessel where blood travels through the body from the heart

artificial heart - a mechanical device designed as a replacement (either temporarily or permanently) for a non-functioning heart

atrium - one of the two upper chambers of the heart, its primary purpose is to receive blood from the veins

capillaries - The body's tiniest blood vessels, they transport blood between the arteries and the veins to all the body's cells

cardiac - related to the heart

cardiac arrest - The cessation of the heartbeat and cardiac function, ending circulation of the blood and often resulting in death

cardiovascular - related to the heart and blood vessels

heart-lung machine - A device designed to take over the work of the heart during open heart surgery, adding oxygen to blood before blood is returned to the body

transplant - The replacement of a damaged organ with a healthy one

vein - blood vessels which carry blood to the heart

ventricle - one of the two lower chambers in the heart, which pump blood to the lungs and the rest of the body

Index